AF601750

Lessons Learned: Short Stories of Continuity and Resilience

Lessons Learned: Short Stories of Continuity and Resilience

Michele L. Turner

M2

CONTENTS

Dedication

This book is dedicated to my family, and friends who are like family; but, most of all to my parents, Lee and Leona Lowery. Their sacrifices, their encouragement, and their prayers, have helped me to achieve my goals. So much love, so many lessons. I am Thankful. Grateful. Blessed.

Lessons Learned: Short Stories of Continuity and Resilience

"I can be changed by what happens to me. But I refuse to be reduced by it." – Maya Angelou, Poet and Novelist

Publisher: M2
Editor: E. Claudette Freeman, Pecan Tree Publishing

Description

Continuity and Resilience - two words that could track to the same destination, albeit, varied in arrival time. According to Merriam-Webster, the definition for Continuity is "uninterrupted connection, succession, or union." Using this same resource, the definition for Resilience is "an ability to recover from or adjust easily to misfortune or change." While an uninterrupted life, free of misfortune may sound wonderful, it is in the challenges, in the changes, that we learn the greatest lessons. This book has been written with 51 years of personal life experiences, and an overlay of close to 30 years of professional subject matter expertise in managing the continuance of business operations across the globe, come rain or shine. Both aspects have resulted in significant lessons learned and stories of continuity and resilience.

Introduction

From a professional perspective, I was blessed to receive my career passion early on. I chose to use the word receive, as I can't say that I found it (I wasn't necessarily looking), and I don't believe that it was happenstance (I believe in blessings over luck). Received is the right word, as the minute that I was introduced to it, I immediately embraced it full on. I felt like the core of this career choice tied nicely with my values. Values that I grew up with as a preacher's kid. A Mennonite preacher's kid no less, with a faith focused on doing good and helping others. So, what career choice encompasses these values? Disaster Recovery (DR) and Business Continuity (BC). Let me explain...

In this career, there is a need to assist the organization in understanding threats, vulnerabilities, and risks that if realized, would negatively impact the company. (Life translation: are you paying attention?). With that understanding, there is the ability to create plans that could assist in reducing those risks, well ahead of a time of disruption. (Life translation: wishing and hoping is not a plan!) Exercising and testing those plans to validate needed steps and functionality is necessary. (Life translation: ok, did that approach work?) The lessons learned in those exercises are baked into the plans, to strengthen the process, and allow the excellent work of the organization to continue, in good times, as well as challenging ones. (Life translation: learn from your mistakes, and keep it moving!). Do good, help others.

Following are stories that have either assisted me in continuing down an identified path or allowed me to choose opportunities for my own resilience. Each chapter reflects significant phases: Prepare, Assess, Remediate, Sustain, and Examine - PARSE. I created this methodology years ago to build out the practice of business continuity in an organization. Through life, both personal and professional, we are constantly parsing information and experiences, dissecting and analyzing for better understanding and continuous improvement. Whether continuing without skipping a beat, or enduring interruptions that take us in a different direction, lessons learned are a part of the story. My hope is that through these stories and lessons learned, you will find a nugget or two to help you parse opportunities in your life and perhaps your organization.

Chapter 1: Prepare–

Fall Seven Times, Stand Up Eight

"Planning is bringing the future into the present so that you can do something about it now." –Allan Lakein, American Author

In the Continuity practice, this first phase addresses steps needed to better prepare the organization to respond effectively to a business interruption. Gaining sponsorship and support, and understanding previous and existing threats, supports our determining where the opportunities lie. Getting buy-in across the board from process owners, to mid management, and senior leadership is critical. Setting the stage for showing the value of Business Continuity to the organization, and then putting the structure in place to manage the program. Remember - If senior leadership doesn't see the value in a program, it is going to go nowhere fast!

From a personal perspective, there were so many people who provided structure to assist in preparing me for this journey called life. One of my earliest sponsors was my Aunt Bernice. Aunt Bernice was a leader in the field of education, and supportive of my but why questions. So much so, that when I asked, "but why can't I go to school yet?" (side note, I was only four), my aunt agreed that I was ready, and she supported the academic exception for me to start kindergarten. Helping me to understand threats and challenges, in stepped my parents: Lee and Leona Lowery (I know, the names, too cute right?). To understand my story, it is important to understand theirs.

Daddy had seen his share of challenges during his youth. Whether being denied service at a diner or being called every name but his own more times than he could count, he leaned on his faith to get through. His father (my grandfather) was a Baptist deacon, and a foreman at the General Motors Corporation. My grandmother was a housewife, and a member of the church, singing in the choir and being active in the community as an Eastern Star (an order focused on biblical examples of working together for good). Grandma and grandpa raised 10 children in their small home in Saginaw, Michigan, all of whom understood the need to share, sacrifice, yet still give to others along the way. This understanding led Daddy to a small Mennonite church in his neighborhood. The Mennonite church has three core values within our confession of faith: 1) Jesus is at the Center of our faith, 2) The Community is at the center of our lives, and 3) Reconciliation is at the center of our work. The people in the church exuded these values. To have a Caucasian pastor, leading an integrated congregation of African American, Caucasian, and a variety of ethnicities, at a time when civil unrest was significant, was quite the story. The religion is a close-knit community. There weren't many African American Mennonites around the country, therefore, when the pastor mentioned that a fellow clergyman in Pennsylvania had spoken of a single, African American woman in his congregation, the Mennonite Connection was on! While a devout Mennonite herself, Momma had also had experience with racial challenges in her rural area of Masontown, Pennsylvania. These challenges were also realized through her own family. Her father (my grandfather) was born of African American and Caucasian parents, and this family history had denied her of meeting half of her family. My grandfather, a strong-willed man, provided for his family by working in the coal mines, underscoring the value of demanding work. My grandmother was right there supporting the family and the community as well. She felt it her duty, to help friends and neighbors in their quest to manage their daily lives whether helping to watch children, cook, or clean clothes. This, with her own full house of six children (three boys, and three girls).

Now, back to Momma and Daddy. With information shared by both pastors, Momma agreed to be introduced to Daddy through correspondence. They wrote letters to each other for three years before meeting. The same afternoon they finally met; Daddy proposed while they walked into town from the train station where he'd arrived. With my grandfather's blessing, they were engaged.

Daddy went back to that little church in Saginaw and years later became the Pastor. And by the way, as of this writing, my parents have been married 57 years and counting.

Their challenges, their learnings, their ability to overcome ugly situations, created beauty in brokenness. The only child of Lee and Leona, the grandchild of James and Estella Lowery, and George and Creola Griffin. Their backdrop of determination, strength, and faith, is what I was born in to.

Lessons Learned:

Personal: The challenges of some who felt that my family was less than, because of the color of our skin was evident. The challenges that my family felt as a result was palpable. Regardless to what was going on around them, my parents had supporters. More so sponsors. The difference is while a supporter will help you along the way and give you elevated level advice directly, a sponsor will extend well past solely the discussions with you, and share wonderful things about you with others.

Looking at what my family has accomplished, through challenges and adversity, through sponsorship, and through faith, I.AM.PROUD. It has prepared me for who I am today. I am because they were, and for that, I am blessed.

Professional: There will be ebbs and flows in the process. The best defense, is a good offense: DO YOUR HOMEWORK, and focus on the three Cs: Clarity, Communication, and Cost.

Clarity: The biggest challenge to be faced is not being distinctively clear on why a program is needed. How would the development of the program underscore the organizational strategies, mission, or vision statement? Show that tie in. In addition, key things to look out for: Were there interruptions that, based on no clear direction, recovery time was extended, or the cost to recover was exorbitant? Was there an audit item called out in the past identifying a gap that has not yet been addressed? Are there regulations that based on the industry, your organization is expected or should align with (view industry links in the Appendix for guidance on current rules and regulations). Were there situations where given no clear plan, customers suffered by not continuing to receive the product or service that you offer? Yes, customers are loyal, however, there is an expectation in return. An expectation that their needs have been considered proactively. Bob Carter, Professor and Head of Earth Sciences at James Cook University called it out: "Poor planning on your part, does not necessitate an emergency on mine." I would add: "And when it does, I'm out."

Communication: One must be precise on how putting a plan in place will assist the organization in being better prepared to respond to business disruptions. In addition, when communicating, point out that the plan isn't just about the what if. As you plan through the process, you will get a better sense of dependencies from one group or service to another. That sense will allow you to make closer connections, potentially streamline processes, and perhaps reduce time to production in the day to day. There will also be an opportunity to better define the relationship between technology and the business. Yes, there is always that discussion about who relies on whom. Reality: One without the other cannot fully support the organization. Being clear on how you plan to answer those questions through this process will be important. You'll need support. You will need senior level representatives from each of the core areas reporting to the C-level, to provide ongoing input and decisioning on the needs and to go forward. Whether it's called a Steering Committee, or a Governance team, having this group hear from their peers, understand the common themes and threads necessary to support an interruption, and perhaps streamline day to day will be important. They can identify points of contacts to connect with to gain insight on the business, critical services, dependencies, needs, etc. Here's the kicker, after the magnificent work that you do to explain why something is needed, you will need to give them a general timeline or roadmap to accomplish it. I get it; you don't know what you don't know. Here's what you do know: You will need to understand current state. You will need to understand risks, priorities of those risks, current mitigations, and the connection points between groups that can facilitate recovery, who needs to do what, when, and where? How do we train these team members? How can we test whether or not our assumptions are correct? There is no magic timeline that states when all of this can be pulled together, this depends on the organization, the culture and clarity on the RACI (Responsible, Accountable, Consulted, and Informed) model. Having a roadmap to identify the timeframe to conduct the risk assessment, recovery solution and plan development, as well as testing will be important to share with leadership.

Cost: At a high-level, there will be costs associated such as software to manage the process and serve as a repository for the data, potential cost of a separate structure to support the recovery process, cost of training materials. Again, no magic number here, however, I go back to the key point:

DO YOUR HOMEWORK on industry software and share initial numbers. Emphasize that this is solely for the purpose of providing insight into potential costs, and the more work the team does in this area, the better they will be able to provide more succinct numbers. Let them know that there will be a check in on progress. You will set up perhaps recurring quarterly meetings to communicate progress against your roadmap, and clarity on costs. This ensures that you gain their buy-in after the needed phases to confirm support. There will be challenges, there will be ebbs and flows. The work that you do is important, stick with it. Remember the three Cs: Clarity, Communication, and Cost

Chapter 2: Assess–

Slow Down To Speed Up

"The hurrier I go, the behinder I get."- Lewis Carroll, Author of Alice in Wonderland.

The Assess phase of the PARSE process has to do with truly identifying critical needs. By conducting a risk assessment, you can determine those areas that could cause or have caused potential challenges within the organization. Understanding the risk, the categorization (high, medium, or low), and those actions needed to mitigate, allows for tactics and controls to be put in place to address the needs. In addition, what some reference as a critical function or business impact analysis, is a process where an organization can identify and prioritize critical services that if not conducted, would negatively impact the successful continuation of the organization. By identifying these functions, dependencies, and resource needs, work arounds or alternate steps can be put in place to continue during not so normal situations.

It's June, almost end of month/end of quarter. Crazy busy. So many things to do, so many things to follow-up on. I've transitioned to manage Business Operations for our Risk group, and I am learning, and I am contributing, and busy,

busy, busy. I've got a full plate, and I lost time taking a family trip to Texas. It was a 22 hour drive there and back. I probably should have helped drive. I passed out as soon as we hit the road, I was so tired. Ridiculously tired! I didn't even wake up for our pit stops. I really haven't been feeling great for the past month or so. Cramps in my chest. I probably just slept the wrong way, too busy to worry about that though; busy, busy, busy. I'm back in the office, have got to catch up, I have a "C" level (CEO, CIO, etc.) meeting first thing tomorrow morning. All the work is done, but I've got to check it twice, three times to make sure. And I've got Arianna's (our daughter) recital tonight; she plays the clarinet, her first recital. So much to do, I still don't feel great, but can't stop, won't stop, busy, busy, busy. I've gone through my list and now I'm rushing to get to the recital on time. The cramps in my chest have gotten harsher and increasingly sharp. So sharp that at times, they take my breath away (must get a new mattress, this old one is killing me). On my way to the recital, I remembered that Momma called. Must call her back, or she will worry. I'm 36 years old, and she still worries as if I'm 16. I've got everything under control, nothing to see here.

"Mickey?" My mind is all over the place, I called Momma but lost in my thoughts, I'm jarred when I hear her voice.

"Hey...Ma."

"Mickey, what's wrong, you don't sound right."

"I'm fine Ma...just busy." My breathing is staggered. I've just got to relax. As soon as I get to the recital, I'll do just that.

"Mickey, is there a clinic by you. Can you stop in?"

"Ma...I'm good. Just need to get... to Anna's (our alternate name for Arianna) recital. Will call...later. Love you, bye." Lord, I'll pay for that. I hung up way too quickly in the middle of her worry. I'll call her later; once I've had a chance to sit. Maybe I should stop. I'm almost there. I just need to try to straighten this cramp/pain out. I arrive at the recital. Parking is crazy. I'm not late, but I'm sure not early. Crap! Where is Oscar? Where are the kids? I'm having difficulty walking. I just need to sit down. Just need to catch my breath. There they are. Midsection, at least I don't have to climb over people to sit. I'm really dizzy, something is wrong. How annoying. Who has time for this? This darn pain. Why is it so difficult to breathe? OK, I give up. I need to get home. I just need to lay down.

"Oscar", I say. "I'm having trouble breathing."

"WHAT?" "WHAT'S GOING ON?"

"Oscar", I say. "We need to get Arianna's attention after her solo, we need to stand up and walk towards the side door, with her in tow, and get home." He's not good with emergencies. We must be organized in our exit! We motion to Anna after her solo, we exit according to plan, and by now, in addition to being short of breath, I can't walk fully upright. Way too painful.

Oscar looks at me. "Get in my car, I'll drive home."

"No way. I would have to leave the car here; I've got too much to do tomorrow." Busy, busy, busy. "I'm driving myself home!" Even I seem a bit stubborn for myself right now, but no matter, I just need to lay down. By the time I made it home, breathing was a true luxury, my chest felt like there was an elephant sitting on it, and there was no way that I was laying down. I might not get back up. “Oscar, take me to the hospital,” I whispered.

“Do I have time to make a sandwich?” The look on my face answered his question, and to the hospital we went. We get there. I needed help to walk, the pain was so intense. I couldn’t answer any questions asked in emergency, and before I knew it, I was being whisked away by EMTs.

“She’s fading. She needs morphine. Who’s on staff?”

“No morphine,” I said. I’ve heard stories of seeing pink elephants and other things with that, I need a clear mind. I’ve got meetings tomorrow.

“We’ve got to get her into x-ray”.

My thoughts: “X- ray? As long as it’s quick. I’ve got things to do.” The doctor is here now. He is saying something, I can’t quite make it out.

“Ms. Turner, you need to be admitted.”

“Oh no, I have too much to do. Can you just give me a pill?”

His look. Somewhat like my earlier one. A mix between concern, annoyance, and urgency. “Ms. Turner, I’m not sure why you are still here - alive I mean. But since you are, do you mind if I do what I need to do to save your life?”

Oh no he didn’t! You just wait. When I am out of this intense pain, and I can see one of him instead of two, I’m writing a letter to someone! The next thing that I remember, I am in CCU being asked to review a medical will. A document to provide direction on what should be done if I don’t make it. A will? I wake up again and I am in a room. Things are fuzzy. I see who I think is my current manager. ”Wait a minute, if

I'm dead Lord, why do you look like my manager?" I fade away again. I was in the hospital for seven days. I celebrated my son's birthday there. I had friends come, with one helping me to break the rules and walk down to the gift shop (I'm such a rebel). Not only did I have a pulmonary embolism, but according to the doctors, my lungs were full of blood clots, and the only place they had left to go was my brain, an aneurysm. I didn't make that meeting, but I was still in the land of the living, and a lot less busy. I was okay with that!

Lessons Learned:

Personal: Really? Was the meeting that important? Important enough to jeopardize my health, my family time, my everything? Anything is possible, but not all at the same time, and not without healthy boundaries? Slowing down is healthy. Think about it, there are brakes on a car, not to ensure that you never move, but to ensure that when you do, you can do so in a controlled way. Pausing when necessary and accelerating when appropriate. I had always been taught that one should have a work/life balance. To be honest, this is what was doing me in. There is no such thing as a work/life balance; not for me anyway. My family will always be my priority, so the attempt to balance is not feasible. My key in this space is harmony and/or integration. This acknowledges that both need to co-exist. A huge part of creating that harmony is also actualizing self-care. Reality: you can't take care of others, if you're twitching somewhere, unable to function, because you have nothing left to give. Conduct your own personal risk assessment: What is the impact of my doing, or not doing "X", what's the likelihood that this impact could occur if this risk were to come to fruition, and yes, what controls can you put in place to mitigate risks that you are susceptible to (overworking, worrying, not taking care of your health, etc.). Get really clear on the controls! Take breaks, take a quick walk, buy a special chair (mine is a red one), that you sit in with a good book, a cup of Earl Grey tea, and a warm fuzzy blanket, and just be. Bottom line for me, I will do what is necessary to integrate my work into my family requirements, but at the end of it all - FAMILY WINS!

Professional: This is the area that can give you clarity on your risk appetite as an organization, as well as an understanding of what services should be prioritized to support an effective recovery or continuation of services. Prior to, identify the scope of the assessment (example: site, state, country). Four things to address: Susceptibility, Plot Assessment, Profile, and Analysis.

Susceptibility: This is going to be different for every organization. The question is: What are the threats/hazards that the organization is most vulnerable to? How likely are these to occur, and what are the impacts when they do? Impact and likelihood are inherent risk. The general definition is that at this state, it is, what it is. Now couple that with an understanding of what controls are in place to mitigate the risk (residual risk), and the detail needed to plot the risk if available. The next step is to document the risks which would result, should this situation come to fruition. (NOTE: For more thorough detail on potential risk categories, please see the COSO detail in the Reference section of the Appendix.)

Plot Assessment: How then can the risk be plotted? Matrices are helpful to provide a visual of where risks sit (High - Red, Medium - Yellow, Low - Green, or We're Set - No Color!). Inherent Risk on the vertical axis, and Residual on the horizontal.

Profile: Whether the decision is made to include all risks noted, or solely the high and moderate, there is detail that will be helpful to track and monitor progress. The cadence for this could be monthly, quarterly, or as determined by the Steering Committee. What are the risks that the organization can accept? What risks, based on impact, must be addressed?

Analysis: We identified up front that there was a need to align the program to the strategy of the organization. This drills down into the strategy of the individual teams as well. There is a need to understand what functions/services support the achievement of those strategies. With that understanding, what dependencies do those functions align to? What resources will be required to ensure that the functions can be completed? When must the functions be brought up in order not to negatively impact the organization (within seconds, minutes, days, etc.)?

Appendix C- #1 provides a template for the above process up through analysis. Think of a threat from your own organization, begin to detail that threat and resulting risk using the direction provided. Plot the risk on the matrix, and then begin to specify the risk detail that can be used to track progress using the risk profile template.

Appendix C-#2 provides a template to document details referenced in the analysis area. All of this helps to understand the risk profile, and the requirements necessary to support the recovery or continuation of the business.

Chapter 3: Remediate–

Your Job Nor Your Current State Defines You

"Don't confuse having a career, with having a life." Hillary Clinton, Former United States Secretary of State

In the Continuity space, Remediate acknowledges the critical functions previously identified, and requests that recovery strategies be put in place to recover these functions, even if you cannot do so at the primary facility. Whether that is to recover at another site, using an alternate approach locally, or regionally, recovery of functions will take place, just in another form. Business will go on.

My daddy called me on September 14th at 7:00am. Not unusual, we talk regularly, but on this day, his words struck a major chord. Even with dementia impacting his thought process, he remains on top of current events. "Mickey," he said (yes, that's my nickname), "the news says that your company will have layoffs today. Will you still have a job?"

"Well, Good Morning Daddy, I'm not at work yet, but I don't think that this will impact me." I had made strong contributions. I'd been there for almost 10 years, moving up the ladder so to speak from Senior Program Manager to

Director, building global programs, and in leadership sessions with visibility across the board. Things happen in corporate, but I should be safe? Right? I did my best to re-assure Daddy that all was good, and then I checked my email. A message from our leadership stating that today would be a rough day, reductions in force would be happening, and we should be thinking of our impacted colleagues at this time. My thoughts: "Of course, this would be rough for them, I will be there for support." Ten minutes later another mail comes across with "do not forward permissions" and a request to meet in a conference room at a designated time. My thoughts: "Ahhhh, they probably want to sequester us while they have conversations with those affected. I will definitely be there for my colleagues."

I arrived in the office and a very somber feel hovered. Silence, no hustle and bustle. No people talking, moving quickly to go to meetings, just silence. My thoughts: "Yes, this will be a rough one." I see my colleague who had been at the company for 20 plus years. There are tears in his eyes. "Michele," he says, "did you get the mail?"

If nothing else, I'm a rule follower, and the mail said not to forward or discuss. "Not sure what you mean." (I am a horrible liar...).

"Michele, if you got a mail to meet in in the conference room at "X" time, you're getting laid off, just like I expect to."

My thoughts: "Oh wow", the pressure is getting to him." I reply, "If I did get a mail, I'm sure that's not what it is." How silly he will feel when he realizes that he is so wrong, and he should just be considering others at this time. I continued,

"I've got work to do, but I will walk with you to the conference room."

"Michele," he says in a loud voice. "Screw the work! We're getting laid off!"

I didn't have time for this, way too many things to do before the meeting. I get a few things done, meet him in the hallway, and we head over. As we walk in the room someone says, "Oh Michele - not you!" My thoughts: "God bless her, she's in the wrong room. I will definitely be there for her when they ask her to step out." I tell my colleague that I want to sit in the front. I want to make sure that I get all the information that I need, to be able to follow guidelines for how to effectively communicate during this time.

He now looks at me worried, "Michele," he says, "when you realize it, look at me and nod your head."

My thoughts: "Here he goes again." Senior leadership comes to the front and immediately comments on how rough of a day it is, and that all in the room have been affected by the reduction in force. I hear it; but I don't. I start to rock. I do this when I'm in deep thought. They then state that they are turning the session over to human resources to discuss severance packages in general. My thoughts: "Severance packages? Wait, something isn't right. Am I in the wrong room?" I begin to tap my nails across each other, I do this when I'm a bit nervous. And then, the piece de resistance, HR states that we can feel free to leave the site today, no need to return. There will be bags over the weekend in a secure area to drop our things off. They ask us to turn around and receive our personalized packages from the representatives in the back of the room. I turn around. WHERE THE HECK DID THEY COME FROM? When I'm extremely upset, I cry out of one eye. Yep – its *Glory* time people (Glory is a great movie by the way). So now I'm rocking, tapping, and crying out of one eye. I'll be lucky if security isn't called. I look over at my colleague and I nod.

The rest is a blur, I remember wanting to finish sending project notes and then realized that was a moot point. I wanted to do it anyway but couldn't focus. I remember thinking, "Drop my things off. My laptop. My badge. BUT THESE ARE MY THINGS!"! I called my husband to let him know. I didn't quite know what to do after that. Applebee's? Yes, that's the ticket. I will drown my sorrows in a burger and a blonde brownie. What had I done, or what didn't I do that brought this on? I was always called upon to speak at events, always looked upon as a key contributor, what happened? Had I made someone mad? Now what? I had wanted to work for this great technology organization since I was a senior in high school, and I did it, and I was successful - until now. Now what? Was I concerned that I wouldn't find another job? No, I was just taken aback that this one had let me go. Reality hit. The same knowledge that I had 10 minutes earlier, the same certifications, the same Industry clout, the same strength - I still had it. I had a mitigation plan, and it was the fact that my knowledge was not just company specific. It could be applied across a variety of industries, and a variety of organizations. Local, alternate site, regional; there were recovery opportunities all around, and I would recover from this event, from this risk, addressing interruptions along the way. That's how I roll!

Lessons Learned:

Personal: A layoff, a reduction in force - this - is - business. Business looks at the bottom line, and other corporate criteria to make these types of hard decisions. I had given so much of myself that I had turned this entity, this "something" into a "someone". This was business, and I had taken it personal. While I made it my job to find another job, I had a tough time reconciling my loss. Yes, loss. Here is what popped me out of it, my 20-year-old daughter. "Mommy," she said, "you always say that you love challenges. Right?"

"Yes, babe, I do," I responded.

"You've said that you always learn something new, and really prove just how strong or knowledgeable you are. Right?"

"Yes, babe, that's true. That's what I believe." Where was she going with this? I feel like I'm being set up.

"Well Mommy, this seems like a challenge, a big one for you, you must be excited about the possibility." Can you put a 20-year-old on punishment? She was right! She was BIG RIGHT! My pride was hurt, but this was a challenge that I could overcome, and overcome I did. I became an instructor for the Disaster Recovery Institute International (DRII), and the rewards of sharing Business Continuity - Professional Practices (located here) with others was amazing. In addition, I went back to that same organization after four months and stayed there another two years until I decided that I would accept a great offer from an amazing e-commerce organization.

Your job, your role at the office, are just a mere portion of the phenomenal person that you are. You ARE so much more. You HAVE so much more. Never forget the many facets of your worth on this journey called life.

Professional: The business continuity professional is in a solid position to see the big picture of the organization, including challenges and risks that could impede progress. With this understanding, the step that remains is to identify what recovery solution may meet the needs of the organization. Three solutions to consider are: Local (work-from-home and an alternate site close in proximity, yet far enough from the affected site), and Remote (geographic redundancy). Listed below are considerations, not an exhaustive list, but items of note:

Local

Work-From-Home: The key is knowing what functions can be done from home, and which cannot. For example- how would the organization feel about providing employees check stock, with a check printer to generate payroll checks? I'm thinking not. To that end, this may be one function that must be done at the organization's site. Other key considerations for this area could be: are there backup contacts noted should the primary resource not be available due to disaster or other. Do all employees identified with a role for recovery or continuation have the necessary equipment? Do they have a laptop, access to the procedures, the necessary permissions and access to systems and software from this site?

Alternate Site: Does the alternate site have the needed equipment and resources to support the critical functions. Is there space available and confirmed for use by the organization? Is a cloud structure in place that must be recognized?

Remote: Should there be a region wide disruption, have regional human resources been trained, with permissions and access to procedures to support requirements? Are there language considerations that were addressed as part of this solution? How does the remote solution map to the follow-the-sun model, meaning are time zones aligned? This is immensely helpful in the case of customer service efforts and being able to immediately have phones answered in alignment with the time zones that the customer is accustomed to?

Remember, to leverage the risk information as scenarios are built out. Scenarios could be weather related, technological, or other. Which categories should be considered for either of the solutions? With all the detail that has been gathered to date, it's time to pull everything together in a plan. Document the purpose, the scope, the teams supporting critical functions, in addition to notification and contact information. DO NOT FORGET VENDOR DETAILS!! Have you inquired about whether they have a plan? Do they know that they are required to support one of the organizations critical functions? Is all clear in terms of the triggers moving from incident (controllable situation) to crisis (out of control and requiring the plan implementation)? Are all clear on the purpose and location of the Emergency Operations Center (EOC), whether virtual or brick and mortar, to ensure that there is a point and process to support decisioning in a crisis situation?

Chapter 4: Sustain–

Putting it to The Test

"Life has many ways of testing a person's will, either by having nothing happen at all or by having everything happen at once." Paulo Coelho, Brazilian Lyricist and Novelist

In the Sustain phase, the documented mitigation strategies are tested. Strategies look great on paper, but do they actually work? In this phase, the tests that are completed, may not be perfect. There will be opportunities for improvement. This is a good thing. Finding these things during a test, versus during an actual disaster, allows for changes to be made. What we tend to find during this time, is a true understanding of what you can, and can't live without.

In 2013, my father was diagnosed with Temporal Lobe Dementia. My hero, the man who, along with my mother, cleaned houses and applied for loans to put me through college at his alma mater was facing a life-altering diagnosis. How did I find out about his condition? I lived in Washington, and my parents still lived in Illinois. My mother called me with a tone of concern in her voice. This was a tone that I hadn't heard before. Even when she suffered from a detached retina that left her blind in one eye, I had never heard this tone.

During this time, she read stories to the church's preschool class. Her blindness threatened to take that away. Rather than disappoint the kids, my father read the stories to her ahead of time, she memorized them, and created felt characters to show the story, as opposed to simply reading it. Her eye ultimately needed to be removed. After surgery, her general comment was, "Well, I guess God will let me in with one eye." When I heard the tone of concern in her voice about my father, I knew that it was not a drill. I caught a flight to Illinois, determined to do my own risk assessment. I landed on a Friday, and by Sunday night, with help from my best friend and her son, I got everything packed up, with the intent to move them in with me. Yes, this was a significant undertaking, but to do this, for my father, for my parents who had done so much for me was a no brainer.

Over the years, there have been learnings. Learning a bit more patience, showing a bit more grace, and of course, communicating with the respect that he deserves as an amazing father. And then COVID-19 happened. All that we had learned over the course of the previous years, would be tested. The best way to describe this is through a blog that I wrote and published in the Alzheimer's Association of Washington and was reprinted in the Disaster Recovery Journal.

<u>Shelters in Places of the Mind</u>

I am not a member of the medical profession, nor am I a scientist who can opine on the inner make-up of the COVID-19 virus. I am a leader in the business resilience industry, with an emphasis on the areas of risk management, emergency response and business continuity. Even so, I am not writing solely to any of those perspectives. I am writing as a person with a loved one who has dementia. A loved one who, while living through this world event where the mantra is "we're in this together," cannot fully connect to this theme. The message just does not resonate with them in the way that it resonates with others.

The reality is that this "new normal" is not normal at all for them. This new normal takes away structures they have become accustomed to, structures they've needed to continue to hold on to. Good, bad or indifferent, the structure of "today" was what helped them through the chaos and inconsistent flashes of "yesterday."

With the uncertainty that is, I am finding that there are ways to help: ways to help which align with my profession, ways that help me to maintain during this time and ways that help me to help them. My three ways are:

Collaboration and connection

We cannot do this alone and we should not do this alone. Having too much to carry leads to stress, especially during this time. An actual slow down, in order to speed up, is what is needed. Anything else is not healthy or productive. Help each other carry the load. Spend more time on the phone with them, video conferencing, talking and sharing the memories that are clear for them. I've found out so much that I didn't know from days gone by, just by listening and connecting.

Celebration

We have to find the areas where we can celebrate the wins. This is critical! If we cannot see progress, discouragement quickly ensues. This leads to nowhere fast. One win that I found just today goes back to technology. My loved one is used to going to church every Sunday, without fail. With COVID-19 and shelter in place, this is just not possible at this time. Win: a new laptop to the rescue! Access to live streaming of the home church services. It may seem like a small win, but the calm that this offers is immeasurable.

Continuity

Where you can find normalcy, hold on to it and drive that continuity. Find a link that will assist in mitigating the reaction or emotional state of today's pandemic, to that of managing the response, based on the plans and processes previously developed. My loved one has always been used to assisting others. Given the condition, this has been difficult, but they find a way. The phone gets a workout! They check on people to make sure that they are okay. That is their Modus Operandi (M.O.). When possible, they do their best to do what is natural for them, what is normal for them, helping guide others in the midst of challenge.

Shelters in Places of the Mind: COVID-19, dementia, and my "loved one"... my dad.

Lessons Learned

Personal: Specifically, the COVID-19 Pandemic has given a cause to pause in our communities. This is an understatement. Pausing, to support our first responders in their call to action to jump in, without question, to do what they were trained to do - HELP OTHERS. Pausing to focus on priorities. Our understanding of what is critical, and what can be deferred has truly been tested. The question then - how can we take the learnings and apply this to our day to day? How can we use this impactful time to build resiliency such that as similar events occur, we can be better prepared to address? How can we use these challenges more as stepping-stones to support the greatness that we could experience as a community?

Professional: Neither exercises, nor tests make perfect, however, they do make the team stronger because of the lessons learned. They strengthen that resiliency muscle to reduce the impact of interruptions that may occur in the future. Whether the process is a walkthrough of the plan against a scenario, or a test to conduct work transference from one site to another, where validation of volumes and procedures take place, the value is significant. This is an opportunity to identify necessary improvements in a safe environment. An opportunity to track gaps. Gaps in recovery time (actual versus planned), and gaps in process (are there single points of failure). Two key phases (outside of execution): 1) Planning and 2) Debrief and Lessons Learned.

Planning: A few things to consider: 1) provide notification to key stakeholders not involved in the exercise or test. This is necessary to ensure that no one misconstrues the test as an actual disaster. 2) ensure that the scenario is realistic. The less realistic, the more credibility will be lost. The scenario should include injects from the business, as this provides an opportunity to engage them and include situations related to their risks and/or challenges. This will allow the participants to realize the value, and 3) be specific about objectives and roles. The objectives will provide clarity on what was accomplished. In addition to the participants and the facilitator, the roles should include a scribe to focus on capturing notes that may not have been documented by the participants. The latter can be leveraged to support the final lessons learned document.

Debrief and Lessons Learned

It will be important to conduct a debriefing after the exercise to gain immediate feedback from the participants, as well as ensure that a general survey is completed to measure success, steps most helpful, and areas of improvement.

While the full lessons learned document includes an Executive Summary, Scope, and Assumptions. It will be important to get clear on the objectives. In addition, documenting action items by category will be helpful to be clear on the core focus areas necessary to improve the plan and process. NOTE: Appendix C- section 3 includes a template for this section of the document.

Chapter 5: Examine–

Continuous Process Improvement

"Life is a process of becoming, a combination of states we have to go through. Where people fail is that they wish to elect a state and remain in it. This is a kind of death." Anais Nin, French-Cuban American diarist, essayist, novelist

PARSE cannot be spelled without an "E"; thus, we get to the last phase, Examine. In this phase, all that we have learned is embedded into the culture of the organization. (Life translation: our core values). Business Continuity is a program, not a project. A project has a beginning and an end, and yes, I know we are not immortal beings, so there will be an end; however, I still align life with a program focus. A program allows for continuous process improvement. The more you know, the more you grow. If we are not growing, then what?

I used to think that growth represented getting new insights, more knowledge, becoming smarter. This is an aspect of growth; however, over the years I have learned that true growth is shown by how you apply that knowledge and enhance not only yourself, but others. This chapter is more reflective in nature, reminding myself of those special times in my life when this was underscored, where nuggets shared with me elevated my thinking, and where based on feedback, and I have elevated others.

Lessons Learned

Personal: SST- Service Study Trimester at Goshen College. Here, I taught English in an orphanage for French girls in Guadeloupe, in the French West Indies. I received more than I gained (including learning how to say curse words in Creole). "You get to travel? Where do you go? What have you learned? How is the U.S.? Do you know Michael Jackson?" These questions, innocent and sincere, may have seemed simple, or even naïve, however, they wanted to know, so they asked. Certain words came out garbled as they practiced their English, but they tried, not one of them gave up. The goal was to learn and apply that learning daily.

Professional: How are you embedding your learnings? How are you showing your values and continuing to include them in everything that you do? I developed and managed the Governance council at a previous organization. Here I worked with the CIO, direct reports, and subject matter experts to discuss metrics and dashboards, and the progress that we were making as an organization. Ahead of one of our sessions, the CIO said to me, "Michele, I don't want to see any watermelons on these charts. I had absolutely NO IDEA what he was talking about. I brought cookies for our break, no fruit (luckily, I only thought this, I didn't say it). Seeing confusion on my face, he broke it down for me: "I don't want to see metrics that are green on the outside to the team, but red on the inside inherently." Rest assured, I shared the message and began asking probing questions as not to have watermelons in my meetings. "This metric has been green for the past three months. Is this one that we should be tracking? How does this assist in our progressing over time?" "This metric went from green to red in a couple of days, what were the leading indicators that could have pointed us to issues earlier, so that we could have escalated and gained more assistance before it all fell apart? "

Share the challenges, without doing so, you cannot get the help that you need, in the time that it's needed to make the difference. If you wait to try to solve it on your own and something goes blazing red, options are limited, more frustration ensues, and it's a rough road across the board. Accept the insight. A leader does not mean that you are the only one that can drive success. A leader knows how to engage others, how to bring others along, and how to help to bring out the best.

For me, the goodness of Business Continuity and of Life for that matter, is that you never stop learning. Learning is not a one and done. There will always be opportunities to apply the previous learning to a new situation that occurs and build from there. What I am challenging myself, and you with, is applying the wonderful things that we've learned, in normal times, as well as disasters. We can gain so much more, if we share what we have, rather than keep it under wraps.

Chapter 6: BONUS "E"!!! Education–

It's Never Too Late

"The time for action is now. It's never too late to do something." Antoine de Saint-Exupery, French Writer, Aviator, Poet and Author

While PARSE is only spelled with one "E", let's add another one - just because. This one stands for Education. As mentioned in Chapter 4, my parents cleaned houses to put me through college. That was the first go 'round. I went directly to college, Goshen College, my father's Alma Mater, after I graduated high school in 1987. For background, my father went back to college the year that I started seventh grade. We moved to Goshen, Indiana so that he could attend the college and achieve his Bachelor in Theology. He had two years at Hesston College, a Mennonite school in Kansas, and decided to close it out at Goshen, a Mennonite liberal arts college. Since it was his Alma Mater, it was somewhat of a foregone conclusion that I would go there as well. My original major was International Business, with a minor in Music Theory. My sophomore year, this changed to a major in Teaching, with a minor in French. By the time my junior year came around, after my SST experience, I decided that I no longer wanted my parents to clean houses and take loans to put me through school. I did work on campus and had a brief stint at McDonalds and cold calling for the local newspaper. Those jobs took care of the Taco Bell addiction that my best friend and I had developed, but that's about it. Even with my decision to leave and go back home to Chicago, I knew that I would not be giving up on my education. I would just defer it a bit until I could pay for it myself. And then life set in. I got married in 1991. Still determined to get my degree, I enrolled in Harold Washington College in downtown Chicago. I took night and weekend classes, however, the onsey-twosey, here and there was taking FOREVER! Two years later, we had our first child, Arianna. I had moved from being a senior receptionist at a bank downtown, to being a senior secretary, then background investigator, and ultimately a business recovery specialist at a financial organization in Northbrook. This latter role was one that I was asked to take when my colleague went on maternity leave. Serving in the position would change the course of my professional career. What started as helping and color-coding documents in a business recovery plan (pink for team information, yellow for vendor details), led to my taking on the role full time. I had so many recommendations for improvement that management decided to offer me the position when my colleague chose not to return. There were many opportunities to learn in my four-year career there. I was indeed hooked on the practice of Business Recovery (process oriented), to have it evolve into full-fledged Business Resumption, I would need to couple it with the practice of Disaster Recovery (technology oriented). I moved on to a technology consulting firm in Chicago, where I rode the bench for a while. No one really wanted to hire someone to document a plan for the what-ifs, not realizing that it could also help with the day to day. For me to begin with a client, I needed to get better at understanding technology quickly. I studied AS400s, networks, routers, server diagnostics, Network Attached Storage, Storage Area Networks, watching and optimizing data packet flow, until I was hired to manage these aspects across a variety of organizations. Once I was in, I got to have real fun, and assist them in developing their business continuity plan to recover their critical services supporting their organizational strategy, develop a plan to protect their systems and ultimately response procedures to protect their most critical asset - their employees. There was so much going on that I wasn't getting many classes in; however, in 1998, after the birth of our second child, Cameron, I decided to push until I finished. With that, in 2000, with my husband sick at home, I drove downtown to Roosevelt University, with my one and a half year old, my seven year old, and my mom, and I walked across the stage, and received my diploma. And received it with Television mogul and publisher Oprah Winfrey looking on! Yes, OPRAH WINFREY!! It just so happened that that her assistant was graduating that same year and she was the commencement speaker. I will never forget her speech. She asked all 675 degree candidates, "What do you know for sure?" She shared that each of us has a calling, and whether we knew it or not, it was up to us to find out what that calling was, and get to the business of doing it. I knew for sure that I had a lot to do in life. I was supposed to learn stuff, do stuff. Do good, help others. Three years passed, and Elijah, our son came along. I had moved from the consulting firm, to a storage area network company, as a network engineer, and later as a vice president within a financial organization. In all these instances, I had the opportunity to help in planning, and executing the plan when disasters and crises would strike. It took another 12 years before I would obtain my Master of Science degree in, you guessed it, Business Continuity. Oprah, if you're reading this; thank you. I answered the call.

Lessons Learned

Personal: Just like my father, I realized that it was never too late to do what needed to be done. He was 44 when he went back to college, I was 42 when I went to get my Master's degree. There could have been many excuses for not going back including "what if I fail". Reality: In whatever failure we have, we've just learned another option that doesn't work, which will lead us to one that does. I went back to school, not for the promise of a promotion, but the promise to myself to continuously strive, and continuously learn not just for myself, but also to help others. Take the Risk. Give back, to help move others forward.

Professional: NEVER STOP LEARNING! In this industry, there are so many places to go to gain more insight. Appendix A has a list of sites that contain information on Continuity and Resilience. Appendix B has links to articles and webinars that may also be of assistance. Networking is critical. Engaging with people who are going through similar challenges, or perhaps different ones that you can gain insight from before you hit that pothole. If you don't know, ask. If you do know, share.

"For what it's worth: it's never too late or, in my case, too early to be whoever you want to be. There's no time limit, stop whenever you want. You can change or stay the same, there are no rules to this thing. We can make the best or the worst of it.

I hope you make the best of it. And I hope you see things that startle you. I hope you feel things you never felt before. I hope you meet people with a different point of view. I hope you live a life you're proud of. If you find that you're not, I hope you have the courage to start all over again."- F. Scott Fitzgerald, American Novelist.

Chapter 7: Upward and Onward

"The horizon leans forward, offering you space to place new steps of change."- Maya Angelou, Poet and Novelist

Prepare, Assess, Remediate, Sustain, Examine- PARSE, with a side of Education. All of these have been brought together to build a structure, not just for the what if, but a structure that allows the organization, which allows the individual, to have a better understanding of the current state.

So, what now? How do we take the lessons that we've learned, and ensure that we use them as a ramp to continuous growth not just for ourselves, but for others? Continue to Speak Up, Take the Risk, Stay Connected.

Speak Up

I can remember being in meetings, new to the organization or that team, and waiting to share my thoughts because, well, I was the newbie and I wanted to process things more before I spoke. The frustration came, when I would hear some of the things, ideas, recommendations that I was thinking, spoken by other people. I had to speed up my process game! I had to trust myself to know that what I had to say was important, and that doing so was my job. That is why I had a seat at that table. I belonged there. Once I became comfortable with that, I spoke out more, I shared more, and more opportunities began to come my way. I had done the prep work, the planning, and I was ready.

Take the Risk

There will be times when you may be presented with an opportunity that makes you a bit nervous, maybe even scares you just a smidge. Take yourself through a mini risk review. What's the impact if you do "X"? What is the impact if you don't do "X"? Will the pros far exceed the cons? How likely is the opportunity to roll its way back to you if you bypass it? What controls have you put in place to hit a home run? Use that data to take the calculated risk as warranted. I took a risk on sitting in for my colleague all those years back. I could have said, "No, this is going to impact my job, never mind." I was curious, I was ready for a new opportunity, and this looked like one that could be interesting. Almost 30 years later, I've been able to learn, and teach domestically and internationally on a topic that I thoroughly enjoy.

Stay Connected

I am proud to say that many of the relationships that I had at the onset of my career; I still have them. I still reach out with inquiries, and for those that I have trained or have been on my teams, they know that they can reach out to me as well. Do not underestimate the value of networking and building relationships. I had a situation where a Corporate Vice President helped me to garner a connection with a Board of Directors member to speak at one of our Affinity group meetings. Through that meeting, and continued conversations, he became my mentor, and one of the people who wrote a letter of recommendation for me as I applied to my Master's degree program at Norwich University. These connections, both personal and professional have assisted me throughout my career, throughout life. Assisted me in realizing that next opportunity, and for that I am grateful. I look at my grandchildren and I see the promise on the horizon for them. I am committed to helping them parse through life and realize the greatness that I know they will achieve.

Continuity and Resilience - two words that could track to the same destination albeit, varied in arrival time. What have you learned along the way that has created the opportunity for you to continue in certain areas without skipping a beat? Conversely, what have you learned along the way that has created those steppingstones, those muscle strengtheners that allow you to get back up after you've been down? Those things are what you should share! Share the experiences, the imperfections, the lessons. Be the catalyst to help others, and yourself. These lessons learned are what are needed to take us all to another level of awareness, another level of growth, and another level of resilience.

Appendix

1. **Reference Sites**

   Association of Continuity Professionals: https://acp-international.com/

   Business Continuity Institute: https://www.thebci.org/

   Committee of Sponsoring Organizations of the Treadway Commission (COSO): https://www.coso.org/Pages/default.aspx

   Coordinating Continuity and Resilience Today: https://www.crtcon.ca/home.html

   Disaster Recovery Institute International: https://drii.org/

   Disaster Recovery Journal: https://drj.com/

   DRJ Rules and Regulations: https://drj.com/resources/dr-rules-and-regulations/

   Emergency Management Advisory Committee: https://www.kingcounty.gov/depts/emergency-management/emergency-management-professionals/emergency-management-advisory-committee.aspx

   Homeland Security Emergency Management: Center of Excellence: https://www.coehsem.com/

Risk and Resilience Hub: https://www.riskandresiliencehub.com/#
The Conference Board: Business Continuity and Crisis Management Council: https://conference-board.org/councils/business-continuity-and-crisis-management

2. **Author Articles and Podcasts**
The Evolution of Cyber Attacks, Evolving with the Times, Michele Turner, October 19th, 2018: https://risk-and-compliance-management.enterprisesecuritymag.com/cxoinsight/the-evolution-of-cyber-attacks-evolving-with-the-times-nid-1427-cid-6.html
Business Resilience Decoded with Vanessa Mathews: Managing Business Resiliency via Geographic Redundancy Strategies: Michele Turner, November 20th, 2018: https://drj.com/decoded/2018/11/20/managing-business-resiliency-via-geographic-redundancy-strategies/
The Continuity Forecast: #24: Yes, You Do Need to Spend Time on Your Business Continuity Plan...Here's 5 Reasons Why w/ Michele Turner, Michele Turner, November 19th, 2019: https://podcasts.apple.com/us/podcast/24-yes-you-do-need-to-spend-time-on-your-business-continuity/id1445580696?i=1000457223125
ALZWA Blog, Shelters in Places of the Mind, Michele Turner, April 8th, 2020: https://alzwablog.org/2020/04/08/shelters/
Disaster Recovery Journal, Shelters in Places of the

Mind, Michele Turner, May 4th, 2020: https://drj.com/journal/shelters-in-places-of-the-mind-covid-19-and-dementia/

3. **Helpful templates**

a. **Sample Assessment log and Risk Profile detail**

<u>Susceptibility (1-3)</u>

<u>High: 3, Medium: 2, Low: 1</u>

Threat	Likelihood and Rating	Impact and Rating			Inherent Risk Rating (Impact X Likelihood)	Controls and Residual Rating	Resulting Risk(s) should this come to fruition
	Highly- 3 Moderate- 2 Low- 1	Customer 3- Regional Impact 2- Country 1-State	Regulatory 3- Fees & Disclosure 2- Fees 1-None	Operational (systems & services) 3- 76%-100% 2-50%-75% 1—0%-49%		1- None 2- Adhoc 3- Repeatable	
							Plot #1
							Plot #2

<u>Plot Assessment</u>

<u>High: Red, Medium: Yellow, Low: Green, We're Set! No color</u>

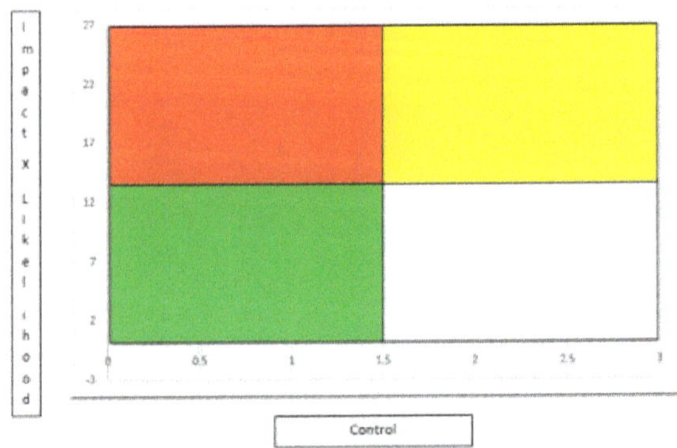

Risk Profile

Threat and Risk	Categorization	Description	Risk Drivers	Impact Detail	Mitigation Actions	Monthly Trending (Up, Down, Stable)	Action Owner	Timeframe for Completion

b. Sample Analysis table

Critical Function/Service and timeframe for recovery and data restoration (Recovery Timeframe Objective and Recovery Point Objective respectively)	Description and critical times per month, quarter, year, etc....	Impact if not conducted	Primary Location	People Resources required per day					Equipment and Software Necessary					Work-around
				1	5	10	15	30+	1	5	10	15	30+	

c. Sample Objectives and Action Item templates

Exercise Objectives	*Met*	*Not Met*
*1. **Walk through** a scenario that acknowledges stakeholder actions to be addressed during a business interruption:*		
- Notification		
- Activation		
- Procedures		
- Close Out		
*2. **Identify gaps** and associated actions.*		
*3. **Document** lessons learned and action items to be leveraged for plan update.*		

Action Items			
Category	*Issue and Description*	*Recommended Action Item*	*Owner(s) and Target Time Frame*

About The Author

Michele L. Turner, MBCP, FBCI, CISA, CRISC, GRCP, has close to 30 years of experience in the areas of Governance, Risk, and Compliance, with a Masters of Science degree in Business Continuity from Norwich University. She is the Head of Global Business Resiliency for Amazon. In this role, she has developed the framework and methodology for Business Continuity, providing leadership for this team, Crisis Management and Resiliency Management (inclusive of Workplace Resiliency) within Amazon's Corporate environment. Prior to this, she led Governance, Risk, Compliance and Business Continuity roles within Microsoft, initiating the Operational Risk Management vertical for the organization. Turner is an international speaker on the topic of Business Continuity, Risk Management, and related areas. She is a requested guest lecturer at the University of Washington, on such topics as Cyber Security and Operational Risk, and a course instructor and board director for Disaster Recovery Institute International (DRII). She provides input as a Director of Giving within that organization's foundation and is also a member of the Conference Boards' Business Continuity and Crisis Management Council.

Michele is a resident of Snohomish, Washington, and an enormously proud grandmother of two amazing grandsons.

"If you want to go fast, go alone. If you want to go far, bring others along." Author unknown, African Proverb.

www.ingramcontent.com/pod-product-compliance
Ingram Content Group UK Ltd.
Pitfield, Milton Keynes, MK11 3LW, UK
UKHW021011290726
14059UKWH00005BA/152/J